ISLAND OF SECRETS: A TALE OF FRIENDSHIP AND ADVENTURE

"UNCOVERING THE ISLAND'S SECRETS LED TO A MYSTERY BEYOND THEIR WILDEST IMAGINATION"

SANAT CHADDHA

Made with ♥ on the Notion Press Platform
www.notionpress.com

Contents

Characters

*1. **Sarah** - A brave and curious girl who loves exploring new places.*

*2. **Max** - A smart and resourceful boy who always thinks outside the box.*

*3. **Alex** - A timid and shy boy who learns to overcome his fears.*

*4. **Lily** - A bubbly and adventurous girl who always sees the bright side of things.*

Other Characters

Mr. Jones, Bill,** and **Maria

Preface

Island of Secrets: A Tale of Friendship And Adventure *is a story that takes young readers on a thrilling journey to a magical island filled with hidden treasures and mysterious creatures. It is a tale of bravery, teamwork, and discovery that will captivate readers of all ages.*

In this story, we follow the journey of Sarah, Max, Alex, and Lily, four young adventurers who find themselves stranded on an island after their boat crashes in the midst of a storm. With the help of their captain, Mr. Jones, they embark on a quest to navigate the island, overcome their fears, and unlock the secrets that it holds.

As the group works together to solve puzzles, face dangerous creatures, and uncover hidden treasures, they learn the true value of friendship and the power of teamwork. But what they don't realize is that the island holds a mystery that will lead them on an unexpected journey beyond their wildest imagination.

Join Sarah, Max, Alex, and Lily as they take you on an adventure of a lifetime, filled with mystery, magic, and the importance of friendship.

Foreword

Island of Secrets: A Tale of Friendship And Adventure is a captivating story that will take young readers on an exciting journey of discovery, teamwork, and friendship. This book is a perfect read for children aged 10 to 16, who love to embark on thrilling adventures and explore new worlds.

In this story, you will join Sarah, Max, Alex, and Lily as they set off on a sailing trip with Mr. Jones. Little do they know that their journey will take them to a mysterious island filled with strange creatures, hidden treasures, and unexpected challenges. As the group navigates through the island, they must overcome their fears, work together, and solve puzzles to unlock the island's secrets.

Island of Secrets is more than just a tale of adventure. It's a story about the power of teamwork and the importance of friendship. Through their journey, Sarah, Max, Alex, and Lily learn to appreciate their individual strengths and differences, and they form lifelong bonds that will stay with them forever.

This book will not only entertain and inspire young readers, but it will also teach them valuable life lessons. So sit back, relax, and get ready to embark on a thrilling adventure with Sarah, Max, Alex, and Lily on the Island of Secrets.

CHAPTER ONE

The Storm

Sarah, Max, Alex, and Lily, four close friends who shared a love for adventure and the open sea, had eagerly been waiting for their upcoming sailing trip with Mr. Jones for several weeks, excitedly counting down the days until they could finally embark on the trip they had been planning and preparing for with meticulous care and attention to detail for many long months, and they were finally ready to set sail.

As the boat sailed away from the harbor, Sarah, Max, Alex, and Lily looked out at the ocean and were amazed by its beauty. The sun was shining bright, and the water was very calm. The four friends were all very happy and smiling a lot as they thought about all the fun and exciting things they would experience on their adventure.

However, as the friends settled into their journey, they noticed that the sky was starting to get darker on the horizon. The wind began to blow stronger, and the waves in the water started to get bigger and stronger, making the boat rock back and forth more than before

Mr. Jones quickly realized that they were headed into a storm. He yelled at the friends to grab their life jackets and hold on tight. The boat was rocking back and forth, and they were all struggling to keep their balance.

Suddenly, the wind started to make a loud howling sound, and heavy rain began to pour down from the sky. Thunder rumbled loudly, and lightning flashed brightly in the dark sky, making the friends feel frightened and scared. However, Mr. Jones, the experienced sailor who was leading the trip, helped to calm them down by reassuring them that they would be able to make it through this difficult weather.

Suddenly, a massive wave hit the boat. The friends were thrown off their feet, and everything went black.

When Sarah regained consciousness, she found herself lying on a sandy beach that she did not recognize. She felt confused and disoriented but managed to sit up and look around. To her surprise, she noticed that the rest of her friends from the sailing trip were also lying on the shore next to her, groaning and moaning in pain. They all seemed to be disoriented and in a state of shock, just like Sarah.

Sarah attempted to get up on her feet, but she felt dizzy, and her legs felt wobbly. She soon realized that they had been washed up onto a small island. As she looked around, she felt a sinking feeling in her chest because she couldn't see the boat that they had been sailing on. It was nowhere to be seen, and the group appeared to be stranded on the island.

Sarah quickly went to the others and tried to wake them up. Max was the first to stir. He looked around, bewildered, and asked what had happened.

Alex and Lily woke up soon after. They all looked at each other, confused and scared. They had no idea how they had ended up on the island or what had happened to Mr. Jones.

They tried to gather their bearings and realized that the island was beautiful, with tall trees, colorful flowers, and chirping birds. However, they had no food or water and didn't know how to survive on the island.

Sarah took charge and suggested that they explore the island to see if they could find any resources that could help them survive. Max agreed, and the group set off to explore the island. They walked along the beach, hoping to find signs of civilization or rescue. However, they soon realized that they were alone on the island.

As the sun began to set, the group knew they needed to find shelter for the night. They searched the island and found a small cave hidden on the side of a hill. It wasn't much, but it was better than nothing. They settled into the cave, tired and scared, but determined to survive.

Sarah tried to keep everyone's spirits up by reminding them that they were strong and capable of finding a way to get off the island and back home. However, Sarah couldn't shake the feeling that there was something more to the storm that brought them to the island.

The group stayed together, huddled in the cave, facing an uncertain future. They knew that they would have to work together and remain calm if they were to survive. They didn't know what lay ahead, but they were determined to face it together.

As they sat in the cave, tired and scared, the group knew that they needed to find a way to escape the island. They didn't know how long they would be stranded or what challenges they would face. But they were determined to stay strong and work together to overcome whatever obstacles came their way.

CHAPTER TWO

The Island

The sun started to rise, and the birds were singing, waking up the four friends who had slept in a cave. They were sore from sleeping on the hard ground. They knew they had to be optimistic and focus on surviving.

Sarah suggested exploring the island to find food and water sources, and the group agreed. They started walking inland, away from the shore. They saw plants and trees they had never seen before, like palm trees, bamboo, wild berries, and fruits.

Sarah, who had studied botany, identified which plants were edible and which were not. They collected some fruits, nuts, and berries to take back to the cave. They found a small stream and drank fresh water, feeling refreshed and energized. But they knew they had to purify the water before drinking it.

As they kept exploring, they discovered a small hut in a

clearing. The hut seemed abandoned, but it was still standing. Sarah knocked on the door, but no one answered. They peeked through the windows and found some useful things inside: fishing equipment, a compass, and a map of the island.

They decided to stay near the hut and built a fire. They used some of the fishing gear to catch fish from the nearby stream, cooked it, and shared the meal. They discussed their next steps and realized they needed to find a way off the island. They looked at the map and saw that the island was much bigger than they thought.

The next day, they set out again, walking for hours, taking breaks to rest and drink water. They climbed hills and crossed rivers but found nothing of use. They were starting to lose hope. As the sun began to set, they decided to head back to the hut.

But as they were walking, they saw a light flickering in the distance. They rushed towards it, excited at the possibility of finding other people. They found a campfire and two people next to it: a man and a woman. They approached cautiously, and the man and woman welcomed them to the campfire, introducing themselves as Bill and Maria.

Bill and Maria were stranded on the island for a long time. They had been on a boat when a big storm came and made their boat sink. They managed to swim to the island and built a small shelter with whatever they could find. They had been living there ever since, trying to survive with limited resources.

When the four friends found Bill and Maria, they were very happy to see other people on the island. They had been alone for a while and were starting to feel hopeless. Bill and Maria welcomed the group to their campfire and they all started talking.

Bill and Maria were very friendly. They told the group about how they managed to survive on the island. They showed them their shelter and the things they had collected. They had found some useful tools and materials on the island, like pieces of driftwood and old fishing nets.

The group was impressed by how resourceful Bill and Maria were. They had managed to make the best out of a bad situation. They had even caught some fish and cooked it on the campfire. The group shared their own experiences and talked about their plans to survive and find a way off the island.

As the night went on, the group started to feel more comfortable around Bill and Maria. They laughed and told stories, enjoying each other's company. But Sarah couldn't shake the feeling that something was off. She couldn't explain why, but she felt like Bill and Maria were hiding something.

Sarah tried to ignore her suspicions and enjoy the moment. But as the night wore on, she couldn't help but observe their behavior. Bill and Maria seemed a little too relaxed, almost too comfortable being stranded on the island. They didn't seem as worried about finding a way off the island as the group was.

Sarah decided to talk to the others about her suspicions. She didn't want to accuse Bill and Maria of anything, but she thought it was important to be cautious. The others listened to Sarah and agreed that they should be careful.

As they settled in for the night, the group felt tired but content. They were surrounded by the sounds of the island: the rustling of leaves, the chirping of crickets, and the distant sound of waves crashing against the shore. They felt safe and secure in the shelter, knowing that they were not alone on the island. They fell asleep, exhausted but happy, dreaming of the adventures that lay ahead.

CHAPTER THREE

The Magical Cave

Bill and Maria were great guides, and they showed the group the best places to find food and water on the island. They led them to a freshwater stream where they could drink and bathe, and they showed them how to find fruits and nuts that were safe to eat.

As they explored the island, the group was amazed by its beauty. Colorful birds and butterflies were flying around, and they saw exotic animals they had never seen before, such as monkeys and iguanas.

The group worked together to gather supplies and build a shelter. They used branches and leaves to construct a sturdy hut that would protect them from the elements. It wasn't a luxurious place, but it was enough to keep them safe and dry.

As they settled into their new home, they started to feel more comfortable on the island. They even started to enjoy their new way of life, away from the stresses of the modern world. They spent their days fishing, exploring, and enjoying the beauty of the island.

One day, as they were walking along the beach, they stumbled upon a cave. It was hidden by the rocks, and it looked like no one had ever been there before.

The group decided to explore the cave, curious about what they might find inside. As they entered the cave, they noticed that it was much larger than they had expected. The walls were covered in sparkling crystals, and the air was filled with a strange, mystical energy.

As the group walked deeper into the cave, they were surprised to see a beautiful, glowing gemstone in the center of the cave. It was as big as a Football and shone in the light, almost like a beacon calling out to them.

Curious, they approached the gemstone, marveling at its beauty. As they got closer, they noticed that it was emitting strange energy, and they felt as though it was trying to communicate with them.

Suddenly, the gemstone began to glow even brighter, and they felt as though they were being transported to another world. They closed their eyes, and when they opened them again, they found themselves standing in the middle of a magical forest.

The group was stunned. They had no idea where they were or how they had gotten there. But they knew that they needed to explore this new world and find a way back home.

As they began to walk through the forest, they saw strange creatures they had never seen before. There were unicorns and centaurs, fairies and elves. They were amazed at the beauty of this new world and the magic that seemed to surround them.

As they walked, they came across a clearing with a beautiful castle in the center. The castle was made of shining white stone, and it looked like it was straight out of a fairy tale.

The group approached the castle, and they were greeted by a beautiful princess. She explained that she was the ruler of this magical kingdom, and she had been waiting for them.

The princess explained that the gemstone in the cave was a magical artifact, and it had the power to transport people to other worlds. She had been waiting for someone to find the gemstone and use it to come to her kingdom.

The group was amazed. They had never believed in magic before, but now they were standing in the middle of a magical kingdom. They were grateful to have found this new world, but they knew that they needed to find a way back home.

The princess offered to help them find a way back home and revealed that the only way to return to their world was to retrieve a special crystal that had been lost for many years. The crystal was said to be located in a magical cave, deep within the heart of the kingdom.

Determined to find the crystal and return home, the group set out on a journey through the kingdom. They traveled through enchanted forests and crossed treacherous rivers, facing challenges they had never encountered before.

Finally, they arrived at the entrance of the magical cave. The entrance was hidden behind a waterfall, and the group had to find a way to get through the water without getting wet.

With the help of the princess, they found a magical flower that could keep them dry even as they passed through the waterfall. They used the flower to pass through the waterfall, and as they emerged on the other side, they saw a long tunnel leading deep into the heart of the cave.

The tunnel was dark, but as they walked deeper into the cave, they saw a faint glow in the distance. The glow grew brighter and brighter until they reached a large chamber filled with glowing crystals of every color.

In the center of the chamber was the crystal they had been searching for. It was a beautiful, glowing crystal that shone like a star. They were about to grab the crystal when they heard a growling noise coming from the shadows.

Suddenly, a fierce dragon appeared, blocking their path to the crystal. The dragon was massive, with scales as black as coal and eyes that glowed like fire.

The group was scared, but they knew they had to fight the dragon if they wanted to retrieve the crystal and return home. Amidst the chaos of the battle, Bill and Maria found themselves facing a massive dragon, and despite their valiant efforts, the overwhelming power of the beast proved to be too much for them, ultimately leading to their demise.

The group fell silent, their hearts heavy with grief. Lily wept openly, while Max clenched his fists in frustration. Alex was too shocked to speak, and Sarah bowed her head in respect. They knew that Bill and Maria had fought bravely, and their sacrifice would never be forgotten. As they mourned their loss, the group vowed to honor their memory by continuing the fight against the dragons and restoring peace to their land.

After a fierce battle, they were able to defeat the dragon and claim the portal.

The group knew that they needed to honor Bill and Maria's memory in a meaningful way. They decided to hold a funeral service, gathering in a special place where they could pay their respects and say goodbye. They buried Bill and Maria's bodies in a peaceful meadow, surrounded by the beauty of nature that they had fought so hard to protect. As a final tribute, the group created a memorial in their honor, a place where they could come and remember the bravery and sacrifice of their fallen friends. The memorial stood as a testament to their enduring friendship and the bond that they had shared, even in the face of great danger.

They said goodbye to the princess and her magical kingdom, promising to return someday.

As they stepped through the portal, they felt themselves being transported back to the cave. They opened their eyes and found themselves standing in front of the gemstone once again.

The group was relieved to be back in but was very sad about

Bill and Maria's demise as they meant a lot to the group.

CHAPTER FOUR

WORKING TOGETHER

As the group returned from the magical kingdom and stepped out of the cave, they were greeted by the sight of a beautiful sunset. The colors in the sky were vibrant, and the clouds seemed to be dancing in the air.

The group had been through so much already on this island, and they had discovered something incredible in the magical cave. But they knew that they still had work to do if they were going to survive and find a way off the island.

They decided to take a walk along the beach to clear their heads and talk about their next steps. As they walked, they noticed that the waves seemed to be getting bigger and more violent.

Before they knew it, a massive wave crashed onto the shore, sending them tumbling into the water. They struggled to keep their heads above water, but the waves were too strong.

They were being pulled out to sea, and they knew that they had to find a way to get back to shore. They swam as hard as they could, but they were getting tired.

Just as they were about to give up hope, they saw a small island in the distance. They swam towards it, using all their strength to reach the shore.

When they finally made it to the island, they collapsed onto the sand, exhausted but relieved to be alive. They looked around, and they realized that this island was much smaller than the one they had been on before.

They decided to explore the island to see if they could find any resources or signs of civilization. As they walked along the beach, they saw a small boat washed up on the shore.

They couldn't believe their luck. They had been stranded on the island for so long, and now they had a way to get off it. They inspected the boat, and they saw that it was in good condition, with no damage.

The group decided to make camp on the island and wait for the stormy weather to pass. They knew that they had a chance to get off the island, but they also knew that they needed to be careful. They didn't want to take any unnecessary risks and jeopardize their chance of survival.

As they settled into their new surroundings, they discovered that the island was home to a variety of wildlife. They saw birds, lizards, and even monkeys swinging through the trees.

One day, as they were exploring the island, they stumbled upon a small cave hidden in the rocks. They decided to investigate, curious about what they might find inside.

As they entered the cave, they saw something that made their hearts race. The walls were covered in sparkling diamonds and precious gemstones. There were rubies, emeralds, and sapphires, all shimmering in the light.

The group couldn't believe their luck. They had found a treasure trove, and they knew that this could be their ticket off the island. They collected as many gemstones as they could carry and made plans to use them to buy their way onto a passing ship.

But as they were leaving the cave, they heard a strange noise coming from the darkness. They froze, unsure of what to do.

Suddenly, a figure emerged from the shadows. It was a man, dressed in ragged clothes and carrying a large bag.

The man looked at the group with suspicion, and he demanded to know what they were doing in the cave. They explained that they had stumbled upon it by accident, but the man didn't believe them.

He accused them of trying to steal his treasure, and he lunged at them with a knife. The group was caught off guard, and they struggled to defend themselves against the crazed man.

Finally, they were able to overpower him, and they tied him up. They knew that they needed to get off the island as soon as possible, but they couldn't.

As the group sat by the campfire on the small island, they discussed what to do with the man they had captured in the cave. He was still tied up, and they had been keeping a close eye on him, unsure of what he might do.

They decided to question him about the treasure in the cave, hoping to find out if there was more to it than they had initially thought. The man was hesitant at first, but after some convincing, he revealed that he had been living on the island for years, and he had been the one to discover the cave.

He told them that the treasure was cursed and that anyone who tried to take it would suffer a terrible fate. The group was skeptical, but they couldn't ignore the eerie feeling they got from the cave.

They decided to leave the man on the island and take the boat to the nearest town to see if they could find someone to buy the gemstones from them. They hoped that they could use the money to buy passage on a ship and finally get off the island.

As they sailed towards the town, they encountered another storm. This one was even worse than the last, and they struggled to keep the boat afloat. But they were determined to reach their destination and sell the gemstones, no matter what.

Finally, after days at sea, they reached the town. They were exhausted, but they felt relieved to have made it safely. They headed straight to the market to sell the gemstones, but they quickly realized that it wasn't going to be as easy as they had hoped.

The gemstones were of high quality, but they were also rare, and the merchants in the town were suspicious of their origins. They didn't want to buy stolen goods, and they were hesitant to trust the group.

After several failed attempts, they finally met a merchant who was willing to buy the gemstones, but only for a fraction of their value. The group was disappointed, but they knew that they didn't have many options.

They sold the gemstones and used the money to buy passage on a ship. They were finally leaving the island, and they felt a sense of relief and excitement.

As they sailed away from the island, they looked back at it one last time. They couldn't help but wonder what other secrets it held, and they felt a pang of regret for leaving so much unexplored.

But they were also glad to be leaving behind the danger and uncertainty of the island. They were ready for a new adventure, one that didn't involve storms, mysterious caves, or cursed treasure.

As they sailed toward their next destination, they felt a sense of peace and contentment. They had been through so much together, and they had formed a strong bond that would last a lifetime.

But their sense of peace was short-lived. As they sailed through the night, they heard a strange noise coming from below deck. They went to investigate and found that the man they had left on the island had stowed away on the ship.

He had escaped from his bindings and was holding a knife, looking more desperate and crazed than ever. The group knew that they were in trouble, and they quickly tried to disarm the man.

But he was quick and agile, and he fought back with a ferocity that surprised them. They struggled to subdue him, and in the chaos, the ship ran aground on a rocky shore.

The group was thrown from the ship and washed up on the shore, battered and bruised. They looked around, disoriented, and saw that they were on another island, one that was even more mysterious and foreboding than the last.

They knew that they were in for another adventure, one that would test their strength, courage, and friendship. They didn't know what secrets this island held

CHAPTER FIVE

The Map

Once the group had washed up on the shore of the new island, they were disoriented and confused. They had no idea where they were or what had happened to the man they had left behind.

After much discussion, the group agreed to explore the island in search of any clues or resources that could help them. They knew that they needed to be cautious, as they had already encountered danger on the previous island, but they also knew that they couldn't just sit and wait for rescue.

As they explored the island, they came across a dense forest that seemed to go on forever. They hesitated at first, but then decided to venture in, hoping to find something useful. The trees were twisted and gnarled, and the ground was covered in a thick layer of mist that made it hard to see more than a few feet in front of them.

After they had walked for what seemed like hours, the group was exhausted and desperate for a break. Just when they thought they couldn't take another step, they stumbled upon a small clearing. In the center of the clearing stood a tree that looked unlike any they had ever seen before. Its trunk was twisted and gnarled, and its leaves were a deep shade of purple. As they approached the tree, they noticed a small chest lying at its base. They couldn't believe their luck - it was like the tree and the chest had been put there just for them. With trembling hands, they approached the chest and slowly lifted the lid.

As they opened the chest, they discovered an old, worn map lying inside. Even though it was hard to see because of the fading and damage, they recognized that it was a map of the islands surrounding them. The map showed the location of many different places they had never heard of before, and some of them looked like they could be incredibly interesting to explore. They examined the map closely, trying to decipher the names of the places and the routes they could take to get there. It was clear that this map could lead them to great discoveries and adventures. They decided to keep the map and use it to guide them on their journey.

The group felt incredibly happy and excited when they found the old map because they realized that it could be their way off the island. They had been stranded on the island for a while and were starting to lose hope of finding a way back home. However, the map gave them new hope and renewed their determination to find a way out. They knew that if they could use the map to find the right path, they could discover new places and possibly find someone who could help them leave the island. The group was thrilled to have a new goal to work on.

As they studied the map, they noticed that there were several islands nearby, and they began to plot their course. They knew that they had to be careful, as they had limited resources, but they were determined to find a way off the island.

They spent the next few days gathering supplies and preparing for their journey. They built a small raft, hoping that it would be enough to get them to the nearest island.

As they set off on their journey, they encountered many challenges. The sea was rough, and they were constantly battling against the waves. They were also running low on food and water, and they knew that they had to find land soon.

Finally, after what seemed like an eternity, they spotted land in the distance. They rowed towards it, and as they approached, they could see that it was a lush tropical island, with dense foliage and towering trees.

As they stepped onto the sandy beach, they felt a sense of relief wash over them. They had made it to the next island,

and they knew that they were one step closer to finding a way off the island chain.

They spent the next few days exploring the island, searching for any clues or resources that could help them. They discovered a freshwater stream and a variety of fruit trees, which provided them with much-needed sustenance.

As they were exploring the island, they came across an old hut. It was small and dilapidated, but upon closer inspection, they discovered that it was filled with all sorts of treasures.

They found old maps, weapons, and even a small boat, which they realized could be their ticket off the island chain. They knew that they had to be careful, as there could be others on the island who might try to steal their newfound resources.

As they were about to leave the hut, they noticed a strange marking on one of the maps. It was a small island that was marked with an X. They realized that this could be the key to finding their way off the island chain.

CHAPTER SIX

The Enchanted Forest

The group of survivors set out on their small boat, using the map they had found to navigate their way to the mysterious island marked with an X. As they sailed closer, they could see that the island was covered in a dense forest, unlike any they had ever seen before.

As they entered the forest, they immediately felt a strange energy surrounding them. The trees seemed to shimmer with a magical glow, and they could hear whispers in the wind. They knew that they had entered an enchanted forest, filled with mystery and danger.

As they ventured deeper into the forest, they came across a small clearing. In the center of the clearing stood a beautiful fountain, with water that sparkled in the sunlight. The group approached the fountain, and as they did, they felt a sudden burst of energy.

They realized that the fountain was enchanted, and it had given them all magical abilities. One member of the group could control fire, another could create ice, and another had the power to levitate objects. They were amazed by their newfound abilities, but they also knew that they had to be careful, as they could attract unwanted attention.

As they continued to explore the forest, they came across a group of creatures unlike any they had ever seen before. They were small, with wings that shimmered in the sunlight. The group was hesitant at first, but they soon realized that the creatures were friendly and wanted to help them on their journey.

The creatures led the group to a small cottage, where they met an old woman who seemed to have magical powers of her own. She told them that she had been waiting for them and that she knew of their quest to find a way off the island chain.

She gave them a warning, however. She told them that the island they were searching for was guarded by a powerful enchantress, who would stop at nothing to keep them from leaving. She also told them that the enchantress had the power to control the minds of anyone who entered her domain and that they would need to be careful if they wanted to make it out alive.

The group was nervous, but they knew that they had come too far to turn back now. They thanked the old woman for her help and set out once again into the forest.

As they journeyed further, they could feel the power of the enchantress growing stronger. They could hear her whispers in the wind, and they could feel her influence in their minds. They knew that they had to be careful, as they did not want to fall under her spell.

Finally, they arrived at the entrance to the enchantress's domain. They could see that it was guarded by a powerful spell, and they knew that they would need all of their magical abilities to break through.

Using their powers, they managed to break the spell and enter the domain. They could feel the enchantress's power all around them, but they were determined to find a way off the island chain.

As they journeyed through the domain, they came across all sorts of magical creatures, some friendly and some not. They battled their way through the domain, using their powers to fend off the enchantress's minions.

Finally, they came to the center of the domain, where the

enchantress stood waiting for them. She was beautiful and powerful, and she had the power to control their minds.

But the group was strong, and they used their magical powers to battle the enchantress. They fought for what seemed like hours, and finally, they emerged victorious.

As they left the domain, they could feel the enchantress's power fading away. They knew that they had broken her hold on the island chain, and they knew that they had found a way off the island.

As they sailed away from the enchanted forest, they could feel a sense of relief and accomplishment.

CHAPTER SEVEN

The Final Challenge

The group of survivors sailed away from the enchanted forest, relieved and exhausted from their battle with the Enchantress. As they sailed towards their next destination, they couldn't help but feel a sense of unease. They had escaped the island chain, but they were still lost at sea.

After several days of sailing, they finally spotted land in the distance. As they approached, they could see that it was a small island, covered in lush greenery and surrounded by crystal-clear waters. They decided to dock their boat and explore the island, hoping to find some clues as to where they were.

As they explored the island, they came across a small village, filled with friendly locals. They asked the locals if they knew where they were, and the villagers told them that they were on the Island of the Ancients, a mysterious island that was said to hold great power.

The group was intrigued, and they asked the villagers to tell them more about the island. The villagers told them that the island was once home to a powerful civilization, known as the Ancients. The Ancients were said to have possessed great magical powers, and they used their powers to build incredible structures and protect the island from outsiders.

The villagers warned the group that the island was dangerous and that the ruins of the Ancient civilization were filled with traps and puzzles that could be deadly. But the group was determined to explore the island, and they set out to uncover its secrets.

As they explored the island, they came across a massive structure, unlike anything they had ever seen before. The structure was made of stone, and it towered above the trees, its walls covered in strange markings and symbols.

The group decided to investigate, and they entered the structure. As they walked through the halls, they could feel the energy of the Ancients all around them. They could hear whispers in the wind, and they could feel the power of the island growing stronger.

As they explored deeper, they came across a room filled with strange artifacts. One of the artifacts caught their eye, a small statue made of pure gold. As they picked up the statue, they could feel a sudden burst of energy. They realized that the statue was enchanted, and it had given them all new abilities.

One member of the group could now control the elements, another could communicate with animals, and another had the power of teleportation. They were amazed by their new abilities, and they knew that they would need them if they were to uncover the secrets of the island.

As they continued to explore, they came across a massive chamber, filled with strange machinery and devices. They could feel the power of the Ancients growing stronger, and they knew that they were close to uncovering the island's secrets.

But as they approached the center of the chamber, they were suddenly attacked by a group of creatures, unlike anything they had ever seen before. The creatures were made of metal, and they moved with incredible speed and agility.

The group battled the creatures, using their new abilities to fend them off. But the creatures were relentless, and they seemed to be growing stronger with each passing moment.

Finally, the group managed to destroy the last of the creatures, but they were exhausted and injured. As they lay on the ground, they could feel the energy of the Ancients fading away.

They realized that they had stumbled upon something incredible, something that could change the course of history. But they also knew that they had to be careful, as the power they had uncovered could attract unwanted attention.

As they left the chamber, they could feel a sense of accomplishment, but also a sense of unease. They knew that they had uncovered something incredible, but they also knew that they had entered into something dangerous.

As they sailed away from the Island of the Ancients, they wondered what other secrets the island held, and what dangers they would have to face in the future.

CHAPTER EIGHT

Going Home

As the group sailed away from the Island of the Ancients, they knew that they had uncovered something incredible, but they also knew that they had to be careful. They had to keep the power they had found a secret, or it could fall into the wrong hands.

They sailed for several days, keeping a low profile and staying hidden from other ships. But as they neared the coast of a new island, they noticed a group of ships on the horizon, sailing towards them.

The group was nervous, but they knew they had to face the ships head-on. As they drew closer, they saw that the ships were heavily armed and manned by a group of pirates.

The pirates demanded that the group surrender their ship and all their belongings. But the group refused, knowing that they couldn't let the pirates get their hands on the powerful artifacts they had found on the Island of the

Ancients.

The pirates attacked, and the group fought back fiercely, using their newly acquired powers to gain the upper hand. But the pirates were skilled fighters, and the battle was intense.

Finally, the group managed to defeat the pirates, but their ship had taken a lot of damage in the fight. They needed to find a safe place to dock and repair their ship.

They sailed towards the nearest island, a lush tropical paradise filled with tall palm trees and crystal clear waters. As they docked their ship, they were greeted by friendly locals who offered to help them repair their ship.

The group was grateful for the help, and they decided to explore the island while their ship was being repaired. As they walked through the lush forest, they came across a beautiful waterfall, surrounded by colorful flowers and exotic birds.

As they approached the waterfall, they noticed a strange symbol carved into the rocks. The symbol was unlike anything they had seen before, and they knew that it must have some kind of magical significance.

They decided to investigate further, and they followed the trail that led behind the waterfall. As they entered the cave, they could feel the energy of the island growing stronger. They could hear whispers in the wind, and they could sense a powerful force at work.

They continued through the cave, following the symbols carved into the walls. Finally, they came to a large chamber, filled with strange devices and machines.

In the center of the chamber, they saw a massive transparent crystal, glowing with a bright blue light. They knew that this crystal was the source of the island's power, and they knew that they had to be careful. Inside the transparent crystal, there seemed a thing like an old map.

But as they approached the crystal, they were suddenly attacked by a group of shadowy figures. The figures moved with incredible speed, and they seemed to be made of pure darkness.

The group fought back fiercely, using their powers to fend off the shadowy figures. But the figures were relentless, and they seemed to be growing stronger with each passing moment.

Finally, the group managed to destroy the last of the shadowy figures, but they were exhausted and injured.

They knew that they had uncovered something incredible, something that could change the course of history.

As they left the chamber, they knew that they had to be careful. They had uncovered a powerful force, and they knew that others would come looking for it.

They knew that they had to keep the power they had found a secret. They had to protect it from those who would use it for evil. As they started sailing away from the island the crystal broke into two parts, and there came a map from inside the crystal. To their amazement, the map showed the way to their homes. They were very excited to go to their respective homes after such a long time.

CHAPTER NINE

The Secret Message

As the group sailed away from the island, excited to go to their homes, they were still reeling from their encounter with the shadowy figures.

As they sailed through the open sea, they noticed a bottle floating in the water. Curious, they fished it out of the water and found a message inside.

The message was written in an ancient language, one that none of them could read. They knew that it must be important, so they decided to find someone who could help them translate it.

They sailed towards the nearest port and asked around for someone who could translate the ancient language. Finally, they were directed to an old sage who lived in a small hut on the outskirts of town.

The sage was hesitant at first, but when he saw the message, he grew excited. He told the group that the message was a map of a lost city, a city that was said to hold great power and treasure.

The group was intrigued and decided to follow the map. They sailed towards the location marked on the map, and after several days of sailing, they arrived at a small island.

The island was deserted, and they could see a large temple in the distance. As they approached the temple, they noticed a group of armed men guarding the entrance.

The group was hesitant, but they knew that they had to get inside the temple. They decided to sneak past the guards and make their way inside.

As they entered the temple, they could feel the power of the city pulsing around them. They knew that they were close to uncovering the secrets of the lost city.

But as they explored the temple, they noticed that there were traps and obstacles everywhere. They had to use their wits and their newfound powers to navigate through the maze-like temple.

Finally, they reached the center of the temple, where they found a large chamber filled with gold and precious jewels. But they also found something else, something that made their blood run cold.

In the center of the chamber, they found a statue of a dark god. The statue was alive, and it spoke to them in a language that none of them could understand.

The group was terrified, but they knew that they had to destroy the statue. They used their powers to attack the statue, but it seemed to be invincible.

Finally, they realized that they needed to work together to defeat the statue. They combined their powers, and with a final burst of energy, they destroyed the statue.

As the statue crumbled to the ground, they saw something else hidden inside. It was a small box, and inside the box was a powerful artifact, one that could change the course of history.

The group knew that they had to keep the artifact a secret, or it could fall into the wrong hands. They sailed away from the island, carrying their newfound treasure with them.

As they sailed towards the horizon, they knew that they had uncovered something incredible, something that could change the world. But they also knew that they had to be careful, for the artifact they had found was a secret that could never be shared.

CHAPTER TEN

The Mystery Unfolds

As the group sailed away from the lost city, they couldn't help but feel a sense of unease. They had uncovered a powerful artifact, but they knew that there were others who would stop at nothing to get their hands on it.

They decided to split up and take different routes home, to avoid any potential threats. As they sailed towards their respective homes, they couldn't shake the feeling that they were being watched.

When they finally arrived home, they found that things had changed. Their homes were not as they had left them, and there were signs of a struggle.

They quickly realized that they had been followed and that their secret was not as safe as they had hoped. They knew that they had to act fast before it was too late.

They gathered together and decided to track down their pursuers. They used their skills and powers to follow the trail, and it led them to a secret organization, one that had been searching for the artifact for years.

The organization was powerful, and it had resources that the group could never hope to match. But the group was determined, and they knew that they had to stop the organization from getting their hands on the artifact.

They snuck into the organization's headquarters, and what they found was shocking. The organization was made up of powerful individuals, each with their unique powers and abilities.

But the group had a secret weapon - the artifact. They used their power to defeat the members of the organization, one by one.

As they made their way through the headquarters, they found a room filled with ancient artifacts, each one more powerful than the last. And at the center of the room, they found a mysterious figure, one that they had never seen before.

The figure introduced themselves as the leader of the

organization, and they revealed that they had been searching for the artifact for a very long time. They told the group that the artifact was more powerful than they could ever imagine and that they had to give it to them.

But the group refused, knowing that the organization would use the artifact for their nefarious purposes. They used their powers to fight the leader, but they soon realized that they were no match for them.

Just as they were about to be defeated, the artifact began to glow with an otherworldly light. The light enveloped the group, and they found themselves transported to a new location.

When they looked around, they saw that they were in a strange new world, one that they had never seen before. The artifact had taken them to a place that was beyond their wildest dreams, and they knew that they had uncovered a new mystery, one that would take them on even more incredible adventures.

As the group looked out at the horizon, they knew that their journey was far from over. They had uncovered a powerful artifact, defeated a dangerous organization, and found themselves in a new world. But they also knew that there were more mysteries to uncover, and more dangers to face.

The story ends with the group looking out at the horizon, wondering what incredible adventures awaited them next.

Sarah, Max, Alex, and Lily

The End

9 798889 867753

Printed by Libri Plureos GmbH in Hamburg, Germany